DATE

STARTING POINT

DESTINATION

DISTANCE

DURATION

WEATHER CONDITIONS

WATER VISIBILITY

CLEAR 1 2 3 4 5 MISTY

TEAM / PADDLE PARTNER

·	·
·	·
·	·

BODY OF WATER

☐ LAKE	☐ RIVER	☐ CANAL
☐ SEA	☐ OCEAN	☐ OTHER

GEAR & EQUIPMENT

TRIP GOALS

ROUTE

MILESTONES & STOPS	TIME OF ARRIVAL	HIGHLIGHTS & NOTES

ADDITIONAL NOTES

DATE

STARTING POINT

DESTINATION

DISTANCE

DURATION

WEATHER CONDITIONS

WATER VISIBILITY

CLEAR 1   2   3   4   5 MISTY

TEAM / PADDLE PARTNER

·	·
·	·
·	·

BODY OF WATER

☐ LAKE	☐ RIVER	☐ CANAL
☐ SEA	☐ OCEAN	☐ OTHER

GEAR & EQUIPMENT

TRIP GOALS

ROUTE

MILESTONES & STOPS	TIME OF ARRIVAL	HIGHLIGHTS & NOTES

ADDITIONAL NOTES

DATE

STARTING POINT

DESTINATION

DISTANCE

DURATION

WEATHER CONDITIONS

WATER VISIBILITY

| CLEAR | 1 | 2 | 3 | 4 | 5 | MISTY |

TEAM / PADDLE PARTNER

·	·
·	·
·	·

BODY OF WATER

☐ LAKE	☐ RIVER	☐ CANAL
☐ SEA	☐ OCEAN	☐ OTHER

GEAR & EQUIPMENT

TRIP GOALS

ROUTE

MILESTONES & STOPS	TIME OF ARRIVAL	HIGHLIGHTS & NOTES

ADDITIONAL NOTES

	DATE	

DATE

STARTING POINT

DESTINATION

DISTANCE

DURATION

WEATHER CONDITIONS

WATER VISIBILITY

CLEAR 1 2 3 4 5 MISTY

TEAM / PADDLE PARTNER

•	•
•	•
•	•

BODY OF WATER

☐ LAKE	☐ RIVER	☐ CANAL
☐ SEA	☐ OCEAN	☐ OTHER

GEAR & EQUIPMENT

TRIP GOALS

ROUTE

⚑ MILESTONES & STOPS	🕐 TIME OF ARRIVAL	☆ HIGHLIGHTS & NOTES

ADDITIONAL NOTES

DATE

STARTING POINT

DESTINATION

DISTANCE

DURATION

WEATHER CONDITIONS

WATER VISIBILITY

CLEAR 1 2 3 4 5 MISTY

TEAM / PADDLE PARTNER

·	·
·	·
·	·

BODY OF WATER

☐ LAKE	☐ RIVER	☐ CANAL
☐ SEA	☐ OCEAN	☐ OTHER

GEAR & EQUIPMENT

TRIP GOALS

ROUTE

MILESTONES & STOPS	TIME OF ARRIVAL	HIGHLIGHTS & NOTES

ADDITIONAL NOTES

DATE

STARTING POINT

DESTINATION

DISTANCE

DURATION

WEATHER CONDITIONS

SUN | PARTLY CLOUDY | RAIN | STORM | SNOW

☐ ☐ ☐ ☐ ☐

WATER VISIBILITY

CLEAR | 1 | 2 | 3 | 4 | 5 | MISTY
○ | ○ | ○ | ○ | ○

TEAM / PADDLE PARTNER

·	·
·	·
·	·

BODY OF WATER

☐ LAKE	☐ RIVER	☐ CANAL
☐ SEA	☐ OCEAN	☐ OTHER

GEAR & EQUIPMENT

TRIP GOALS

ROUTE

MILESTONES & STOPS	TIME OF ARRIVAL	HIGHLIGHTS & NOTES

ADDITIONAL NOTES

DATE

STARTING POINT

DESTINATION

DISTANCE

DURATION

WEATHER CONDITIONS

☀ ⛅ ☁ 🌧 ❄

☐ ☐ ☐ ☐ ☐

WATER VISIBILITY

CLEAR 1 2 3 4 5 MISTY
○ ○ ○ ○ ○

TEAM / PADDLE PARTNER

·	·
·	·
·	·

BODY OF WATER

☐ LAKE	☐ RIVER	☐ CANAL
☐ SEA	☐ OCEAN	☐ OTHER

GEAR & EQUIPMENT

TRIP GOALS

ROUTE

🚩 MILESTONES & STOPS	🕐 TIME OF ARRIVAL	☆ HIGHLIGHTS & NOTES

ADDITIONAL NOTES

📅 **DATE**	
STARTING POINT	
🚩 **DESTINATION**	
📍 **DISTANCE**	
⏱ **DURATION**	

WEATHER CONDITIONS

🌡 ____ ☀️ ⛅ 🌧 ⛈ ❄️

🌬 ____ ☐ ☐ ☐ ☐ ☐

WATER VISIBILITY

☀️ | 1 | 2 | 3 | 4 | 5 | ☁️
CLEAR ◯ ◯ ◯ ◯ ◯ MISTY

TEAM / PADDLE PARTNER

•	•
•	•
•	•

BODY OF WATER

☐ LAKE	☐ RIVER	☐ CANAL
☐ SEA	☐ OCEAN	☐ OTHER

GEAR & EQUIPMENT

TRIP GOALS

ROUTE

🚩 MILESTONES & STOPS	🕐 TIME OF ARRIVAL	⭐ HIGHLIGHTS & NOTES

ADDITIONAL NOTES

DATE

STARTING POINT

DESTINATION

DISTANCE

DURATION

WEATHER CONDITIONS

———

———

WATER VISIBILITY

CLEAR 1 2 3 4 5 MISTY

TEAM / PADDLE PARTNER

•	•
•	•
•	•

BODY OF WATER

☐ LAKE	☐ RIVER	☐ CANAL
☐ SEA	☐ OCEAN	☐ OTHER

GEAR & EQUIPMENT

TRIP GOALS

ROUTE

MILESTONES & STOPS	TIME OF ARRIVAL	HIGHLIGHTS & NOTES

ADDITIONAL NOTES

📅 **DATE**	
🛶 **STARTING POINT**	
🚩 **DESTINATION**	
📍 **DISTANCE**	
⏱ **DURATION**	

WEATHER CONDITIONS

🌡 ____ ☀️ ⛅ 🌧 ⛈ ❄️

🪁 ____ ☐ ☐ ☐ ☐ ☐

WATER VISIBILITY

☀️ 1 2 3 4 5 ☁️
CLEAR ◯ ◯ ◯ ◯ ◯ MISTY

TEAM / PADDLE PARTNER

•	•
•	•
•	•

BODY OF WATER

☐ LAKE	☐ RIVER	☐ CANAL
☐ SEA	☐ OCEAN	☐ OTHER

GEAR & EQUIPMENT

TRIP GOALS

ROUTE

🚩 MILESTONES & STOPS	🕐 TIME OF ARRIVAL	⭐ HIGHLIGHTS & NOTES

ADDITIONAL NOTES

DATE

STARTING POINT

DESTINATION

DISTANCE

DURATION

WEATHER CONDITIONS

WATER VISIBILITY

CLEAR 1 2 3 4 5 MISTY

TEAM / PADDLE PARTNER

•	•
•	•
•	•

BODY OF WATER

☐ LAKE	☐ RIVER	☐ CANAL
☐ SEA	☐ OCEAN	☐ OTHER

GEAR & EQUIPMENT

TRIP GOALS

ROUTE

MILESTONES & STOPS	TIME OF ARRIVAL	HIGHLIGHTS & NOTES

ADDITIONAL NOTES

DATE

STARTING POINT

DESTINATION

DISTANCE

DURATION

WEATHER CONDITIONS

WATER VISIBILITY

CLEAR   1   2   3   4   5   MISTY

TEAM / PADDLE PARTNER

•	•
•	•
•	•

BODY OF WATER

☐ LAKE	☐ RIVER	☐ CANAL
☐ SEA	☐ OCEAN	☐ OTHER

GEAR & EQUIPMENT

TRIP GOALS

ROUTE

MILESTONES & STOPS	TIME OF ARRIVAL	HIGHLIGHTS & NOTES

ADDITIONAL NOTES

DATE

STARTING POINT

DESTINATION

DISTANCE

DURATION

WEATHER CONDITIONS

WATER VISIBILITY

CLEAR 1 2 3 4 5 MISTY

TEAM / PADDLE PARTNER

·	·
·	·
·	·

BODY OF WATER

☐ LAKE	☐ RIVER	☐ CANAL
☐ SEA	☐ OCEAN	☐ OTHER

GEAR & EQUIPMENT

TRIP GOALS

ROUTE

MILESTONES & STOPS	TIME OF ARRIVAL	HIGHLIGHTS & NOTES

ADDITIONAL NOTES

DATE

STARTING POINT

DESTINATION

DISTANCE

DURATION

WEATHER CONDITIONS

WATER VISIBILITY

CLEAR 1 2 3 4 5 MISTY

TEAM / PADDLE PARTNER

·	·
·	·
·	·

BODY OF WATER

LAKE	RIVER	CANAL
SEA	OCEAN	OTHER

GEAR & EQUIPMENT

TRIP GOALS

ROUTE

MILESTONES & STOPS	TIME OF ARRIVAL	HIGHLIGHTS & NOTES

ADDITIONAL NOTES

DATE

STARTING POINT

DESTINATION

DISTANCE

DURATION

WEATHER CONDITIONS

WATER VISIBILITY

CLEAR 1 2 3 4 5 MISTY

TEAM / PADDLE PARTNER

·	·
·	·
·	·

BODY OF WATER

☐ LAKE	☐ RIVER	☐ CANAL
☐ SEA	☐ OCEAN	☐ OTHER

GEAR & EQUIPMENT

TRIP GOALS

ROUTE

☆ MILESTONES & STOPS	⏱ TIME OF ARRIVAL	☆ HIGHLIGHTS & NOTES

ADDITIONAL NOTES

📅 **DATE**	
🧭 **STARTING POINT**	
🚩 **DESTINATION**	
📍 **DISTANCE**	
⏱️ **DURATION**	

WEATHER CONDITIONS

🌡️ ____ ☀️ ⛅ ☁️ 🌧️ ❄️

🎏 ____ ☐ ☐ ☐ ☐ ☐

WATER VISIBILITY

☀️ CLEAR — 1 — 2 — 3 — 4 — 5 — ☁️ MISTY

TEAM / PADDLE PARTNER

•	•
•	•
•	•

BODY OF WATER

☐ LAKE	☐ RIVER	☐ CANAL
☐ SEA	☐ OCEAN	☐ OTHER

GEAR & EQUIPMENT

TRIP GOALS

ROUTE

📍 MILESTONES & STOPS	🕐 TIME OF ARRIVAL	⭐ HIGHLIGHTS & NOTES

ADDITIONAL NOTES

DATE

STARTING POINT

DESTINATION

DISTANCE

DURATION

WEATHER CONDITIONS

WATER VISIBILITY

CLEAR 1 2 3 4 5 MISTY

TEAM / PADDLE PARTNER

•	•
•	•
•	•

BODY OF WATER

☐ LAKE	☐ RIVER	☐ CANAL
☐ SEA	☐ OCEAN	☐ OTHER

GEAR & EQUIPMENT

TRIP GOALS

ROUTE

MILESTONES & STOPS	TIME OF ARRIVAL	HIGHLIGHTS & NOTES

ADDITIONAL NOTES

📅 **DATE**	
🧭 **STARTING POINT**	
🚩 **DESTINATION**	
📍 **DISTANCE**	
⏱️ **DURATION**	

WEATHER CONDITIONS

🌡️ _____ ☀️ ⛅ ☁️ 🌧️ ❄️

🏳️ _____ ☐ ☐ ☐ ☐ ☐

WATER VISIBILITY

☀️ CLEAR 1 ○ 2 ○ 3 ○ 4 ○ 5 ○ MISTY

TEAM / PADDLE PARTNER

•	•
•	•
•	•

BODY OF WATER

☐ LAKE	☐ RIVER	☐ CANAL
☐ SEA	☐ OCEAN	☐ OTHER

GEAR & EQUIPMENT

TRIP GOALS

ROUTE

🏁 MILESTONES & STOPS	🕐 TIME OF ARRIVAL	⭐ HIGHLIGHTS & NOTES

ADDITIONAL NOTES

📅 **DATE**	
🧭 **STARTING POINT**	
🚩 **DESTINATION**	
📍 **DISTANCE**	
⏱️ **DURATION**	

WEATHER CONDITIONS

🌡️ _____ ☀️ ⛅ 🌧️ ⛈️ ❄️

🏳️ _____ ☐ ☐ ☐ ☐ ☐

WATER VISIBILITY

☀️ 1   2   3   4   5 ☁️
CLEAR ○   ○   ○   ○   ○ MISTY

TEAM / PADDLE PARTNER

•	•
•	•
•	•

BODY OF WATER

☐ LAKE	☐ RIVER	☐ CANAL
☐ SEA	☐ OCEAN	☐ OTHER

GEAR & EQUIPMENT

TRIP GOALS

ROUTE

🗺️ MILESTONES & STOPS	🕐 TIME OF ARRIVAL	⭐ HIGHLIGHTS & NOTES

ADDITIONAL NOTES

DATE

STARTING POINT

DESTINATION

DISTANCE

DURATION

WEATHER CONDITIONS

WATER VISIBILITY

CLEAR 1 2 3 4 5 MISTY

TEAM / PADDLE PARTNER

•	•
•	•
•	•

BODY OF WATER

☐ LAKE	☐ RIVER	☐ CANAL
☐ SEA	☐ OCEAN	☐ OTHER

GEAR & EQUIPMENT

TRIP GOALS

ROUTE

MILESTONES & STOPS	TIME OF ARRIVAL	HIGHLIGHTS & NOTES

ADDITIONAL NOTES

DATE

STARTING POINT

DESTINATION

DISTANCE

DURATION

WEATHER CONDITIONS

WATER VISIBILITY

CLEAR 1 2 3 4 5 MISTY

TEAM / PADDLE PARTNER

•	•
•	•
•	•

BODY OF WATER

☐ LAKE	☐ RIVER	☐ CANAL
☐ SEA	☐ OCEAN	☐ OTHER

GEAR & EQUIPMENT

TRIP GOALS

ROUTE

MILESTONES & STOPS	TIME OF ARRIVAL	HIGHLIGHTS & NOTES

ADDITIONAL NOTES

DATE

STARTING POINT

DESTINATION

DISTANCE

DURATION

WEATHER CONDITIONS

WATER VISIBILITY

CLEAR 1 2 3 4 5 MISTY

TEAM / PADDLE PARTNER

•	•
•	•
•	•

BODY OF WATER

☐ LAKE	☐ RIVER	☐ CANAL
☐ SEA	☐ OCEAN	☐ OTHER

GEAR & EQUIPMENT

TRIP GOALS

ROUTE

MILESTONES & STOPS	TIME OF ARRIVAL	HIGHLIGHTS & NOTES

ADDITIONAL NOTES

DATE

STARTING POINT

DESTINATION

DISTANCE

DURATION

WEATHER CONDITIONS

WATER VISIBILITY

CLEAR 1 2 3 4 5 MISTY

TEAM / PADDLE PARTNER

•	•
•	•
•	•

BODY OF WATER

☐ LAKE	☐ RIVER	☐ CANAL
☐ SEA	☐ OCEAN	☐ OTHER

GEAR & EQUIPMENT

TRIP GOALS

ROUTE

MILESTONES & STOPS	TIME OF ARRIVAL	HIGHLIGHTS & NOTES

ADDITIONAL NOTES

📅 **DATE**	
🛶 **STARTING POINT**	
🚩 **DESTINATION**	
📍 **DISTANCE**	
⏱️ **DURATION**	

WEATHER CONDITIONS

🌡️ ___ ☀️ ⛅ ☁️ 🌧️ ❄️

🚩 ___ ☐ ☐ ☐ ☐ ☐

WATER VISIBILITY

☀️   1   2   3   4   5   ☁️

CLEAR ○   ○   ○   ○   ○   MISTY

TEAM / PADDLE PARTNER

•	•
•	•
•	•

BODY OF WATER

☐ LAKE	☐ RIVER	☐ CANAL
☐ SEA	☐ OCEAN	☐ OTHER

GEAR & EQUIPMENT

TRIP GOALS

ROUTE

🗺️ MILESTONES & STOPS	🕐 TIME OF ARRIVAL	⭐ HIGHLIGHTS & NOTES

ADDITIONAL NOTES

DATE

STARTING POINT

DESTINATION

DISTANCE

DURATION

WEATHER CONDITIONS

☀ ⛅ 🌧 ⛈ ❄

☐ ☐ ☐ ☐ ☐

WATER VISIBILITY

CLEAR	1	2	3	4	5	MISTY
○	○	○	○	○	○	

TEAM / PADDLE PARTNER

•	•
•	•
•	•

BODY OF WATER

☐ LAKE	☐ RIVER	☐ CANAL
☐ SEA	☐ OCEAN	☐ OTHER

GEAR & EQUIPMENT

TRIP GOALS

ROUTE

MILESTONES & STOPS	TIME OF ARRIVAL	HIGHLIGHTS & NOTES

ADDITIONAL NOTES

📅 DATE	
🧭 STARTING POINT	
🚩 DESTINATION	
📍 DISTANCE	
⏱️ DURATION	

WEATHER CONDITIONS

🌡️ ___ ☀️ ⛅ 🌧️ ⛈️ ❄️

🚩 ___ ☐ ☐ ☐ ☐ ☐

WATER VISIBILITY

☀️ CLEAR 1 ○ 2 ○ 3 ○ 4 ○ 5 ○ ☁️ MISTY

TEAM / PADDLE PARTNER

·	·
·	·
·	·

BODY OF WATER

☐ LAKE	☐ RIVER	☐ CANAL
☐ SEA	☐ OCEAN	☐ OTHER

GEAR & EQUIPMENT

TRIP GOALS

ROUTE

🚩 MILESTONES & STOPS	🕐 TIME OF ARRIVAL	⭐ HIGHLIGHTS & NOTES

ADDITIONAL NOTES

DATE

STARTING POINT

DESTINATION

DISTANCE

DURATION

WEATHER CONDITIONS

WATER VISIBILITY

CLEAR 1 2 3 4 5 MISTY

TEAM / PADDLE PARTNER

·	·
·	·
·	·

BODY OF WATER

| ☐ LAKE | ☐ RIVER | ☐ CANAL |
| ☐ SEA | ☐ OCEAN | ☐ OTHER |

GEAR & EQUIPMENT

TRIP GOALS

ROUTE

MILESTONES & STOPS	TIME OF ARRIVAL	HIGHLIGHTS & NOTES

ADDITIONAL NOTES

DATE

STARTING POINT

DESTINATION

DISTANCE

DURATION

WEATHER CONDITIONS

WATER VISIBILITY

| CLEAR | 1 | 2 | 3 | 4 | 5 | MISTY |

TEAM / PADDLE PARTNER

•	•
•	•
•	•

BODY OF WATER

	LAKE		RIVER		CANAL
	SEA		OCEAN		OTHER

GEAR & EQUIPMENT

TRIP GOALS

ROUTE

MILESTONES & STOPS	TIME OF ARRIVAL	HIGHLIGHTS & NOTES

ADDITIONAL NOTES

DATE

STARTING POINT

DESTINATION

DISTANCE

DURATION

WEATHER CONDITIONS

WATER VISIBILITY

CLEAR 1 2 3 4 5 MISTY

TEAM / PADDLE PARTNER

•	•
•	•
•	•

BODY OF WATER

LAKE	RIVER	CANAL
SEA	OCEAN	OTHER

GEAR & EQUIPMENT

TRIP GOALS

ROUTE

MILESTONES & STOPS	TIME OF ARRIVAL	HIGHLIGHTS & NOTES

ADDITIONAL NOTES

DATE

STARTING POINT

DESTINATION

DISTANCE

DURATION

WEATHER CONDITIONS

WATER VISIBILITY

CLEAR 1 2 3 4 5 MISTY

TEAM / PADDLE PARTNER

•	•
•	•
•	•

BODY OF WATER

☐ LAKE	☐ RIVER	☐ CANAL
☐ SEA	☐ OCEAN	☐ OTHER

GEAR & EQUIPMENT

TRIP GOALS

ROUTE

🗺 MILESTONES & STOPS	🕐 TIME OF ARRIVAL	☆ HIGHLIGHTS & NOTES

ADDITIONAL NOTES

DATE

STARTING POINT

DESTINATION

DISTANCE

DURATION

WEATHER CONDITIONS

WATER VISIBILITY

CLEAR 1 2 3 4 5 MISTY

TEAM / PADDLE PARTNER

·	·
·	·
·	·

BODY OF WATER

☐ LAKE	☐ RIVER	☐ CANAL
☐ SEA	☐ OCEAN	☐ OTHER

GEAR & EQUIPMENT

TRIP GOALS

ROUTE

MILESTONES & STOPS	TIME OF ARRIVAL	HIGHLIGHTS & NOTES

ADDITIONAL NOTES

DATE

STARTING POINT

DESTINATION

DISTANCE

DURATION

WEATHER CONDITIONS

☀ | ⛅ | ☁ | 🌧 | ❄
☐ | ☐ | ☐ | ☐ | ☐

WATER VISIBILITY

CLEAR | 1 | 2 | 3 | 4 | 5 | MISTY

TEAM / PADDLE PARTNER

•	•
•	•
•	•

BODY OF WATER

| ☐ LAKE | ☐ RIVER | ☐ CANAL |
| ☐ SEA | ☐ OCEAN | ☐ OTHER |

GEAR & EQUIPMENT

TRIP GOALS

ROUTE

🚩 MILESTONES & STOPS	🕐 TIME OF ARRIVAL	☆ HIGHLIGHTS & NOTES

ADDITIONAL NOTES

DATE

STARTING POINT

DESTINATION

DISTANCE

DURATION

WEATHER CONDITIONS

WATER VISIBILITY

CLEAR   1   2   3   4   5   MISTY

TEAM / PADDLE PARTNER

·	·
·	·
·	·

BODY OF WATER

☐ LAKE	☐ RIVER	☐ CANAL
☐ SEA	☐ OCEAN	☐ OTHER

GEAR & EQUIPMENT

TRIP GOALS

ROUTE

MILESTONES & STOPS	TIME OF ARRIVAL	HIGHLIGHTS & NOTES

ADDITIONAL NOTES

	DATE	
	STARTING POINT	
	DESTINATION	
	DISTANCE	
	DURATION	

WEATHER CONDITIONS

🌡 _____ ☀ ⛅ ☁ ⛈ ❄

🌬 _____ ☐ ☐ ☐ ☐ ☐

WATER VISIBILITY

☀ CLEAR 1 2 3 4 5 MISTY

TEAM / PADDLE PARTNER

•	•
•	•
•	•

BODY OF WATER

☐ LAKE	☐ RIVER	☐ CANAL
☐ SEA	☐ OCEAN	☐ OTHER

GEAR & EQUIPMENT

TRIP GOALS

ROUTE

MILESTONES & STOPS	TIME OF ARRIVAL	HIGHLIGHTS & NOTES

ADDITIONAL NOTES

DATE

STARTING POINT

DESTINATION

DISTANCE

DURATION

WEATHER CONDITIONS

‒‒‒‒ ☀ ⛅ ☁ 🌧 ❄

‒‒‒‒ ☐ ☐ ☐ ☐ ☐

WATER VISIBILITY

CLEAR 1 2 3 4 5 MISTY

TEAM / PADDLE PARTNER

·	·
·	·
·	·

BODY OF WATER

☐ LAKE	☐ RIVER	☐ CANAL
☐ SEA	☐ OCEAN	☐ OTHER

GEAR & EQUIPMENT

TRIP GOALS

ROUTE

MILESTONES & STOPS	TIME OF ARRIVAL	HIGHLIGHTS & NOTES

ADDITIONAL NOTES

📅 **DATE**	
🧭 **STARTING POINT**	
🚩 **DESTINATION**	
📍 **DISTANCE**	
⏱ **DURATION**	

WEATHER CONDITIONS

🌡 ____ ☀️ ⛅ 🌧 ⛈ ❄️

🚩 ____ ☐ ☐ ☐ ☐ ☐

WATER VISIBILITY

☀️ CLEAR — 1 ○ — 2 ○ — 3 ○ — 4 ○ — 5 ○ ☁️ MISTY

TEAM / PADDLE PARTNER

•	•
•	•
•	•

BODY OF WATER

☐ LAKE	☐ RIVER	☐ CANAL
☐ SEA	☐ OCEAN	☐ OTHER

GEAR & EQUIPMENT

TRIP GOALS

ROUTE

🚩 MILESTONES & STOPS	⏰ TIME OF ARRIVAL	⭐ HIGHLIGHTS & NOTES

ADDITIONAL NOTES

DATE

STARTING POINT

DESTINATION

DISTANCE

DURATION

WEATHER CONDITIONS

WATER VISIBILITY

CLEAR 1 2 3 4 5 MISTY

TEAM / PADDLE PARTNER

·	·
·	·
·	·

BODY OF WATER

☐ LAKE	☐ RIVER	☐ CANAL
☐ SEA	☐ OCEAN	☐ OTHER

GEAR & EQUIPMENT

TRIP GOALS

ROUTE

MILESTONES & STOPS	TIME OF ARRIVAL	HIGHLIGHTS & NOTES

ADDITIONAL NOTES

DATE

STARTING POINT

DESTINATION

DISTANCE

DURATION

WEATHER CONDITIONS

WATER VISIBILITY

CLEAR 1 2 3 4 5 MISTY

TEAM / PADDLE PARTNER

•	•
•	•
•	•

BODY OF WATER

☐ LAKE		☐ RIVER		☐ CANAL	
☐ SEA		☐ OCEAN		☐ OTHER	

GEAR & EQUIPMENT

TRIP GOALS

ROUTE

🏁 MILESTONES & STOPS	🕐 TIME OF ARRIVAL	☆ HIGHLIGHTS & NOTES

ADDITIONAL NOTES

DATE	
STARTING POINT	
DESTINATION	
DISTANCE	
DURATION	

WEATHER CONDITIONS

☀ ⛅ ☁ 🌧 ❄

☐ ☐ ☐ ☐ ☐

WATER VISIBILITY

CLEAR 1 2 3 4 5 MISTY

TEAM / PADDLE PARTNER

·	·
·	·
·	·

BODY OF WATER

☐ LAKE	☐ RIVER	☐ CANAL
☐ SEA	☐ OCEAN	☐ OTHER

GEAR & EQUIPMENT

TRIP GOALS

ROUTE

MILESTONES & STOPS	TIME OF ARRIVAL	HIGHLIGHTS & NOTES

ADDITIONAL NOTES

📅 **DATE**	
🧭 **STARTING POINT**	
🚩 **DESTINATION**	
📍 **DISTANCE**	
⏱ **DURATION**	

WEATHER CONDITIONS

🌡 —— ☀ ⛅ 🌧 ⛈ ❄

🪭 —— ☐ ☐ ☐ ☐ ☐

WATER VISIBILITY

☀ CLEAR   1 ○   2 ○   3 ○   4 ○   5 ○   MISTY

TEAM / PADDLE PARTNER

•	•
•	•
•	•

BODY OF WATER

☐ LAKE	☐ RIVER	☐ CANAL
☐ SEA	☐ OCEAN	☐ OTHER

GEAR & EQUIPMENT

TRIP GOALS

ROUTE

📍 MILESTONES & STOPS	🕐 TIME OF ARRIVAL	⭐ HIGHLIGHTS & NOTES

ADDITIONAL NOTES

DATE	
STARTING POINT	
DESTINATION	
DISTANCE	
DURATION	

WEATHER CONDITIONS

Temperature: _____ ☀ ⛅ ☁ 🌧 ❄

Wind: _____ ☐ ☐ ☐ ☐ ☐

WATER VISIBILITY

CLEAR 1 2 3 4 5 MISTY

TEAM / PADDLE PARTNER

•	•
•	•
•	•

BODY OF WATER

☐ LAKE	☐ RIVER	☐ CANAL
☐ SEA	☐ OCEAN	☐ OTHER

GEAR & EQUIPMENT

TRIP GOALS

ROUTE

MILESTONES & STOPS	TIME OF ARRIVAL	HIGHLIGHTS & NOTES

ADDITIONAL NOTES

📅 **DATE**	
🛶 **STARTING POINT**	
🚩 **DESTINATION**	
📍 **DISTANCE**	
⏱ **DURATION**	

WEATHER CONDITIONS

🌡 ____   ☀️ ⛅ 🌧 ⛈ ❄️

🎐 ____   ☐ ☐ ☐ ☐ ☐

WATER VISIBILITY

☀️ CLEAR   1 ○   2 ○   3 ○   4 ○   5 ○   🌫 MISTY

TEAM / PADDLE PARTNER

•	•
•	•
•	•

BODY OF WATER

☐ LAKE	☐ RIVER	☐ CANAL
☐ SEA	☐ OCEAN	☐ OTHER

GEAR & EQUIPMENT

TRIP GOALS

ROUTE

📍 MILESTONES & STOPS	🕐 TIME OF ARRIVAL	⭐ HIGHLIGHTS & NOTES

ADDITIONAL NOTES

DATE

STARTING POINT

DESTINATION

DISTANCE

DURATION

WEATHER CONDITIONS

WATER VISIBILITY

CLEAR 1 2 3 4 5 MISTY

TEAM / PADDLE PARTNER

.	.
.	.
.	.

BODY OF WATER

☐ LAKE	☐ RIVER	☐ CANAL
☐ SEA	☐ OCEAN	☐ OTHER

GEAR & EQUIPMENT

TRIP GOALS

ROUTE

MILESTONES & STOPS	TIME OF ARRIVAL	HIGHLIGHTS & NOTES

ADDITIONAL NOTES

DATE	
🛶 STARTING POINT	
🚩 DESTINATION	
📍 DISTANCE	
⏱ DURATION	

WEATHER CONDITIONS

🌡 ____ ☀️ ⛅ ☁️ 🌧 ❄️

🎏 ____ ☐ ☐ ☐ ☐ ☐

WATER VISIBILITY

☀️ 1 —— 2 —— 3 —— 4 —— 5 ☁️
CLEAR ○ ○ ○ ○ ○ MISTY

TEAM / PADDLE PARTNER

•	•
•	•
•	•

BODY OF WATER

☐ LAKE	☐ RIVER	☐ CANAL
☐ SEA	☐ OCEAN	☐ OTHER

GEAR & EQUIPMENT

TRIP GOALS

ROUTE

🪧 MILESTONES & STOPS	🕐 TIME OF ARRIVAL	⭐ HIGHLIGHTS & NOTES

ADDITIONAL NOTES

DATE

STARTING POINT

DESTINATION

DISTANCE

DURATION

WEATHER CONDITIONS

☀ ⛅ ☁ 🌧 ❄

WATER VISIBILITY

CLEAR 1 2 3 4 5 MISTY

TEAM / PADDLE PARTNER

·	·
·	·
·	·

BODY OF WATER

☐ LAKE	☐ RIVER	☐ CANAL
☐ SEA	☐ OCEAN	☐ OTHER

GEAR & EQUIPMENT

TRIP GOALS

ROUTE

MILESTONES & STOPS	TIME OF ARRIVAL	HIGHLIGHTS & NOTES

ADDITIONAL NOTES

DATE

STARTING POINT

DESTINATION

DISTANCE

DURATION

WEATHER CONDITIONS

☀ ⛅ ☁ 🌧 ❄

☐ ☐ ☐ ☐ ☐

WATER VISIBILITY

CLEAR 1 2 3 4 5 MISTY
○ ○ ○ ○ ○

TEAM / PADDLE PARTNER

•	•
•	•
•	•

BODY OF WATER

☐ LAKE	☐ RIVER	☐ CANAL
☐ SEA	☐ OCEAN	☐ OTHER

GEAR & EQUIPMENT

TRIP GOALS

ROUTE

MILESTONES & STOPS	TIME OF ARRIVAL	HIGHLIGHTS & NOTES

ADDITIONAL NOTES

DATE

STARTING POINT

DESTINATION

DISTANCE

DURATION

WEATHER CONDITIONS

WATER VISIBILITY

1   2   3   4   5

CLEAR   MISTY

TEAM / PADDLE PARTNER

·	·
·	·
·	·

BODY OF WATER

LAKE	RIVER	CANAL
SEA	OCEAN	OTHER

GEAR & EQUIPMENT

TRIP GOALS

ROUTE

MILESTONES & STOPS	TIME OF ARRIVAL	HIGHLIGHTS & NOTES

ADDITIONAL NOTES

DATE

STARTING POINT

DESTINATION

DISTANCE

DURATION

WEATHER CONDITIONS

🌡 _____   ☀ ⛅ ☁ 🌧 ❄

💨 _____   ☐ ☐ ☐ ☐ ☐

WATER VISIBILITY

	1	2	3	4	5	
CLEAR	◯	◯	◯	◯	◯	MISTY

TEAM / PADDLE PARTNER

•	•
•	•
•	•

BODY OF WATER

☐ LAKE	☐ RIVER	☐ CANAL
☐ SEA	☐ OCEAN	☐ OTHER

GEAR & EQUIPMENT

TRIP GOALS

ROUTE

MILESTONES & STOPS	TIME OF ARRIVAL	HIGHLIGHTS & NOTES

ADDITIONAL NOTES

DATE	
STARTING POINT	
DESTINATION	
DISTANCE	
DURATION	

WEATHER CONDITIONS

☼ 🌤 ☁ 🌧 🌨 ❄

☐ ☐ ☐ ☐ ☐

WATER VISIBILITY

CLEAR 1 2 3 4 5 MISTY

TEAM / PADDLE PARTNER

•	•
•	•
•	•

BODY OF WATER

☐ LAKE	☐ RIVER	☐ CANAL
☐ SEA	☐ OCEAN	☐ OTHER

GEAR & EQUIPMENT

TRIP GOALS

ROUTE

MILESTONES & STOPS	TIME OF ARRIVAL	HIGHLIGHTS & NOTES

ADDITIONAL NOTES

DATE

STARTING POINT

DESTINATION

DISTANCE

DURATION

WEATHER CONDITIONS

WATER VISIBILITY

CLEAR 1 2 3 4 5 MISTY

TEAM / PADDLE PARTNER

•	•
•	•
•	•

BODY OF WATER

☐ LAKE	☐ RIVER	☐ CANAL
☐ SEA	☐ OCEAN	☐ OTHER

GEAR & EQUIPMENT

TRIP GOALS

ROUTE

MILESTONES & STOPS	TIME OF ARRIVAL	HIGHLIGHTS & NOTES

ADDITIONAL NOTES

DATE

STARTING POINT

DESTINATION

DISTANCE

DURATION

WEATHER CONDITIONS

_____   ☼ ⛅ 🌧 ⛈ ❄

_____   ☐ ☐ ☐ ☐ ☐

WATER VISIBILITY

| ☼ | 1 | 2 | 3 | 4 | 5 | ☁ |
| CLEAR | ○ | ○ | ○ | ○ | ○ | MISTY |

TEAM / PADDLE PARTNER

•	•
•	•
•	•

BODY OF WATER

☐ LAKE	☐ RIVER	☐ CANAL
☐ SEA	☐ OCEAN	☐ OTHER

GEAR & EQUIPMENT

TRIP GOALS

ROUTE

🏁 MILESTONES & STOPS	🕐 TIME OF ARRIVAL	☆ HIGHLIGHTS & NOTES

ADDITIONAL NOTES

DATE

STARTING POINT

DESTINATION

DISTANCE

DURATION

WEATHER CONDITIONS

🌡 ____   ☀ ⛅ ☁ 🌧 ❄

🏳 ____   ☐ ☐ ☐ ☐ ☐

WATER VISIBILITY

☀ 1 2 3 4 5 ☁
CLEAR ○ ○ ○ ○ ○ MISTY

TEAM / PADDLE PARTNER

•	•
•	•
•	•

BODY OF WATER

☐ LAKE	☐ RIVER	☐ CANAL
☐ SEA	☐ OCEAN	☐ OTHER

GEAR & EQUIPMENT

TRIP GOALS

ROUTE

MILESTONES & STOPS	TIME OF ARRIVAL	HIGHLIGHTS & NOTES

ADDITIONAL NOTES

DATE

STARTING POINT

DESTINATION

DISTANCE

DURATION

WEATHER CONDITIONS

WATER VISIBILITY

| CLEAR | 1 | 2 | 3 | 4 | 5 | MISTY |

TEAM / PADDLE PARTNER

•	•
•	•
•	•

BODY OF WATER

☐ LAKE	☐ RIVER	☐ CANAL
☐ SEA	☐ OCEAN	☐ OTHER

GEAR & EQUIPMENT

TRIP GOALS

ROUTE

MILESTONES & STOPS	TIME OF ARRIVAL	HIGHLIGHTS & NOTES

ADDITIONAL NOTES

DATE

STARTING POINT

DESTINATION

DISTANCE

DURATION

WEATHER CONDITIONS

WATER VISIBILITY

CLEAR 1 2 3 4 5 MISTY

TEAM / PADDLE PARTNER

•	•
•	•
•	•

BODY OF WATER

LAKE	RIVER	CANAL
SEA	OCEAN	OTHER

GEAR & EQUIPMENT

TRIP GOALS

ROUTE

MILESTONES & STOPS	TIME OF ARRIVAL	HIGHLIGHTS & NOTES

ADDITIONAL NOTES

📅 **DATE**	
🛶 **STARTING POINT**	
🚩 **DESTINATION**	
📍 **DISTANCE**	
⏱️ **DURATION**	

WEATHER CONDITIONS

🌡️ _____ ☀️ ⛅ 🌧️ ⛈️ ❄️

🎐 _____ ☐ ☐ ☐ ☐ ☐

WATER VISIBILITY

☀️   1   2   3   4   5   🌫️

CLEAR ◯ ◯ ◯ ◯ ◯ MISTY

TEAM / PADDLE PARTNER

•	•
•	•
•	•

BODY OF WATER

☐ LAKE	☐ RIVER	☐ CANAL
☐ SEA	☐ OCEAN	☐ OTHER

GEAR & EQUIPMENT

TRIP GOALS

ROUTE

📍 MILESTONES & STOPS	🕐 TIME OF ARRIVAL	⭐ HIGHLIGHTS & NOTES

ADDITIONAL NOTES

📅 **DATE**	
⊕ **STARTING POINT**	
🚩 **DESTINATION**	
📍 **DISTANCE**	
⏱ **DURATION**	

WEATHER CONDITIONS

🌡 ___ ☀️ ⛅ 🌧 ⛈ ❄️

🚩 ___ ☐ ☐ ☐ ☐ ☐

WATER VISIBILITY

☀️ CLEAR 1 ○ 2 ○ 3 ○ 4 ○ 5 ○ MISTY

TEAM / PADDLE PARTNER

•	•
•	•
•	•

BODY OF WATER

☐ LAKE	☐ RIVER	☐ CANAL
☐ SEA	☐ OCEAN	☐ OTHER

GEAR & EQUIPMENT

TRIP GOALS

ROUTE

📍 MILESTONES & STOPS	🕐 TIME OF ARRIVAL	☆ HIGHLIGHTS & NOTES

ADDITIONAL NOTES

DATE

STARTING POINT

DESTINATION

DISTANCE

DURATION

WEATHER CONDITIONS

WATER VISIBILITY

| CLEAR | 1 | 2 | 3 | 4 | 5 | MISTY |

TEAM / PADDLE PARTNER

·	·
·	·
·	·

BODY OF WATER

| ☐ LAKE | ☐ RIVER | ☐ CANAL |
| ☐ SEA | ☐ OCEAN | ☐ OTHER |

GEAR & EQUIPMENT

TRIP GOALS

ROUTE

MILESTONES & STOPS	TIME OF ARRIVAL	HIGHLIGHTS & NOTES

ADDITIONAL NOTES

DATE

STARTING POINT

DESTINATION

DISTANCE

DURATION

WEATHER CONDITIONS

WATER VISIBILITY

CLEAR 1 2 3 4 5 MISTY

TEAM / PADDLE PARTNER

•	•
•	•
•	•

BODY OF WATER

☐ LAKE	☐ RIVER	☐ CANAL
☐ SEA	☐ OCEAN	☐ OTHER

GEAR & EQUIPMENT

TRIP GOALS

ROUTE

MILESTONES & STOPS	TIME OF ARRIVAL	HIGHLIGHTS & NOTES

ADDITIONAL NOTES

DATE

STARTING POINT

DESTINATION

DISTANCE

DURATION

WEATHER CONDITIONS

WATER VISIBILITY

CLEAR 1   2   3   4   5 MISTY

TEAM / PADDLE PARTNER

·	·
·	·
·	·

BODY OF WATER

LAKE	RIVER	CANAL
SEA	OCEAN	OTHER

GEAR & EQUIPMENT

TRIP GOALS

ROUTE

MILESTONES & STOPS	TIME OF ARRIVAL	HIGHLIGHTS & NOTES

ADDITIONAL NOTES

DATE

STARTING POINT

DESTINATION

DISTANCE

DURATION

WEATHER CONDITIONS

☀ ⛅ ☁ 🌧 ⛈ ❄

☐ ☐ ☐ ☐ ☐

WATER VISIBILITY

CLEAR 1 2 3 4 5 MISTY

TEAM / PADDLE PARTNER

•	•
•	•
•	•

BODY OF WATER

☐ LAKE	☐ RIVER	☐ CANAL
☐ SEA	☐ OCEAN	☐ OTHER

GEAR & EQUIPMENT

TRIP GOALS

ROUTE

MILESTONES & STOPS	TIME OF ARRIVAL	HIGHLIGHTS & NOTES

ADDITIONAL NOTES

DATE

STARTING POINT

DESTINATION

DISTANCE

DURATION

WEATHER CONDITIONS

☀ ⛅ ☁ 🌧 ❄

☐ ☐ ☐ ☐ ☐

WATER VISIBILITY

| CLEAR | 1 | 2 | 3 | 4 | 5 | MISTY |

TEAM / PADDLE PARTNER

·	·
·	·
·	·

BODY OF WATER

☐ LAKE	☐ RIVER	☐ CANAL
☐ SEA	☐ OCEAN	☐ OTHER

GEAR & EQUIPMENT

TRIP GOALS

ROUTE

MILESTONES & STOPS	TIME OF ARRIVAL	HIGHLIGHTS & NOTES

ADDITIONAL NOTES

DATE

STARTING POINT

DESTINATION

DISTANCE

DURATION

WEATHER CONDITIONS

WATER VISIBILITY

| CLEAR | 1 | 2 | 3 | 4 | 5 | MISTY |

TEAM / PADDLE PARTNER

•	•
•	•
•	•

BODY OF WATER

☐ LAKE	☐ RIVER	☐ CANAL
☐ SEA	☐ OCEAN	☐ OTHER

GEAR & EQUIPMENT

TRIP GOALS

ROUTE

🏁 MILESTONES & STOPS	🕐 TIME OF ARRIVAL	☆ HIGHLIGHTS & NOTES

ADDITIONAL NOTES

DATE	WEATHER CONDITIONS

DATE

STARTING POINT

DESTINATION

DISTANCE

DURATION

WEATHER CONDITIONS

WATER VISIBILITY

1   2   3   4   5

CLEAR   MISTY

TEAM / PADDLE PARTNER

•	•
•	•
•	•

BODY OF WATER

☐ LAKE	☐ RIVER	☐ CANAL
☐ SEA	☐ OCEAN	☐ OTHER

GEAR & EQUIPMENT

TRIP GOALS

ROUTE

MILESTONES & STOPS	TIME OF ARRIVAL	HIGHLIGHTS & NOTES

ADDITIONAL NOTES

DATE	
STARTING POINT	
DESTINATION	
DISTANCE	
DURATION	

WEATHER CONDITIONS

🌡 _____ ☀ ⛅ ☁ 🌧 ❄

🚩 _____ ☐ ☐ ☐ ☐ ☐

WATER VISIBILITY

☀ 1 2 3 4 5 ☁
CLEAR ○ ○ ○ ○ ○ MISTY

TEAM / PADDLE PARTNER

•	•
•	•
•	•

BODY OF WATER

☐ LAKE	☐ RIVER	☐ CANAL
☐ SEA	☐ OCEAN	☐ OTHER

GEAR & EQUIPMENT

TRIP GOALS

ROUTE

MILESTONES & STOPS	TIME OF ARRIVAL	HIGHLIGHTS & NOTES

ADDITIONAL NOTES

DATE

STARTING POINT

DESTINATION

DISTANCE

DURATION

WEATHER CONDITIONS

☀ ⛅ ☁ ⛈ ❄

☐ ☐ ☐ ☐ ☐

WATER VISIBILITY

CLEAR 1 2 3 4 5 MISTY

TEAM / PADDLE PARTNER

·	·
·	·
·	·

BODY OF WATER

☐ LAKE	☐ RIVER	☐ CANAL
☐ SEA	☐ OCEAN	☐ OTHER

GEAR & EQUIPMENT

TRIP GOALS

ROUTE

MILESTONES & STOPS	TIME OF ARRIVAL	HIGHLIGHTS & NOTES

ADDITIONAL NOTES

DATE	
STARTING POINT	
DESTINATION	
DISTANCE	
DURATION	

WEATHER CONDITIONS

🌡️ _____   ☀️ ⛅ 🌧️ ⛈️ ❄️
🎐 _____   ☐   ☐   ☐   ☐   ☐

WATER VISIBILITY

CLEAR 1 2 3 4 5 MISTY

TEAM / PADDLE PARTNER

•	•
•	•
•	•

BODY OF WATER

☐ LAKE	☐ RIVER	☐ CANAL
☐ SEA	☐ OCEAN	☐ OTHER

GEAR & EQUIPMENT

TRIP GOALS

ROUTE

MILESTONES & STOPS	TIME OF ARRIVAL	HIGHLIGHTS & NOTES

ADDITIONAL NOTES

DATE

STARTING POINT

DESTINATION

DISTANCE

DURATION

WEATHER CONDITIONS

☀ ⛅ ☁ 🌧 ❄

☐ ☐ ☐ ☐ ☐

WATER VISIBILITY

CLEAR	1	2	3	4	5	MISTY
	○	○	○	○	○	

TEAM / PADDLE PARTNER

•	•
•	•
•	•

BODY OF WATER

☐ LAKE	☐ RIVER	☐ CANAL
☐ SEA	☐ OCEAN	☐ OTHER

GEAR & EQUIPMENT

TRIP GOALS

ROUTE

MILESTONES & STOPS	TIME OF ARRIVAL	HIGHLIGHTS & NOTES

ADDITIONAL NOTES

DATE

STARTING POINT

DESTINATION

DISTANCE

DURATION

WEATHER CONDITIONS

WATER VISIBILITY

CLEAR 1 2 3 4 5 MISTY

TEAM / PADDLE PARTNER

•	•
•	•
•	•

BODY OF WATER

☐ LAKE	☐ RIVER	☐ CANAL
☐ SEA	☐ OCEAN	☐ OTHER

GEAR & EQUIPMENT

TRIP GOALS

ROUTE

MILESTONES & STOPS	TIME OF ARRIVAL	HIGHLIGHTS & NOTES

ADDITIONAL NOTES

📅 **DATE**	
🛶 **STARTING POINT**	
🚩 **DESTINATION**	
📍 **DISTANCE**	
⏱️ **DURATION**	

WEATHER CONDITIONS

🌡️ ___ ☀️ ⛅ 🌧️ ⛈️ ❄️

🎐 ___ ☐ ☐ ☐ ☐ ☐

WATER VISIBILITY

☀️ 1   2   3   4   5 ☁️
CLEAR ◯ ◯ ◯ ◯ ◯ MISTY

TEAM / PADDLE PARTNER

•	•
•	•
•	•

BODY OF WATER

☐ LAKE	☐ RIVER	☐ CANAL
☐ SEA	☐ OCEAN	☐ OTHER

GEAR & EQUIPMENT

TRIP GOALS

ROUTE

🚩 MILESTONES & STOPS	🕐 TIME OF ARRIVAL	⭐ HIGHLIGHTS & NOTES

ADDITIONAL NOTES

DATE

STARTING POINT

DESTINATION

DISTANCE

DURATION

WEATHER CONDITIONS

WATER VISIBILITY

CLEAR 1 2 3 4 5 MISTY

TEAM / PADDLE PARTNER

·	·
·	·
·	·

BODY OF WATER

| ☐ LAKE | ☐ RIVER | ☐ CANAL |
| ☐ SEA | ☐ OCEAN | ☐ OTHER |

GEAR & EQUIPMENT

TRIP GOALS

ROUTE

MILESTONES & STOPS	TIME OF ARRIVAL	HIGHLIGHTS & NOTES

ADDITIONAL NOTES

DATE

STARTING POINT

DESTINATION

DISTANCE

DURATION

WEATHER CONDITIONS

WATER VISIBILITY

CLEAR 1 2 3 4 5 MISTY

TEAM / PADDLE PARTNER

•	•
•	•
•	•

BODY OF WATER

☐ LAKE	☐ RIVER	☐ CANAL
☐ SEA	☐ OCEAN	☐ OTHER

GEAR & EQUIPMENT

TRIP GOALS

ROUTE

🚩 MILESTONES & STOPS	🕐 TIME OF ARRIVAL	⭐ HIGHLIGHTS & NOTES

ADDITIONAL NOTES

DATE

STARTING POINT

DESTINATION

DISTANCE

DURATION

WEATHER CONDITIONS

WATER VISIBILITY

CLEAR 1 2 3 4 5 MISTY

TEAM / PADDLE PARTNER

•	•
•	•
•	•

BODY OF WATER

| ☐ LAKE | ☐ RIVER | ☐ CANAL |
| ☐ SEA | ☐ OCEAN | ☐ OTHER |

GEAR & EQUIPMENT

TRIP GOALS

ROUTE

MILESTONES & STOPS	TIME OF ARRIVAL	HIGHLIGHTS & NOTES

ADDITIONAL NOTES

DATE

STARTING POINT

DESTINATION

DISTANCE

DURATION

WEATHER CONDITIONS

WATER VISIBILITY

CLEAR 1 2 3 4 5 MISTY

TEAM / PADDLE PARTNER

•	•
•	•
•	•

BODY OF WATER

☐ LAKE	☐ RIVER	☐ CANAL
☐ SEA	☐ OCEAN	☐ OTHER

GEAR & EQUIPMENT

TRIP GOALS

ROUTE

MILESTONES & STOPS	TIME OF ARRIVAL	HIGHLIGHTS & NOTES

ADDITIONAL NOTES

📅 DATE	
✴ STARTING POINT	
🚩 DESTINATION	
📍 DISTANCE	
⏱ DURATION	

WEATHER CONDITIONS

🌡 _____   ☀ ⛅ ☁ 🌧 ❄

🌬 _____   ☐ ☐ ☐ ☐ ☐

WATER VISIBILITY

☀ CLEAR   1 ○ 2 ○ 3 ○ 4 ○ 5 ○   ☁ MISTY

TEAM / PADDLE PARTNER

•	•
•	•
•	•

BODY OF WATER

☐ LAKE	☐ RIVER	☐ CANAL
☐ SEA	☐ OCEAN	☐ OTHER

GEAR & EQUIPMENT

TRIP GOALS

ROUTE

🚩 MILESTONES & STOPS	⏰ TIME OF ARRIVAL	☆ HIGHLIGHTS & NOTES

ADDITIONAL NOTES

DATE	
STARTING POINT	
DESTINATION	
DISTANCE	
DURATION	

WEATHER CONDITIONS

☀ ⛅ ☁ 🌧 ❄

☐ ☐ ☐ ☐ ☐

WATER VISIBILITY

CLEAR 1 2 3 4 5 MISTY

TEAM / PADDLE PARTNER

•	•
•	•
•	•

BODY OF WATER

☐ LAKE	☐ RIVER	☐ CANAL
☐ SEA	☐ OCEAN	☐ OTHER

GEAR & EQUIPMENT

TRIP GOALS

ROUTE

MILESTONES & STOPS	TIME OF ARRIVAL	HIGHLIGHTS & NOTES

ADDITIONAL NOTES

DATE

STARTING POINT

DESTINATION

DISTANCE

DURATION

WEATHER CONDITIONS

🌡 _____ ☀ ⛅ 🌧 ⛈ ❄

🚩 _____ ☐ ☐ ☐ ☐ ☐

WATER VISIBILITY

☀ CLEAR 1 2 3 4 5 MISTY

TEAM / PADDLE PARTNER

•	•
•	•
•	•

BODY OF WATER

☐ LAKE	☐ RIVER	☐ CANAL
☐ SEA	☐ OCEAN	☐ OTHER

GEAR & EQUIPMENT

TRIP GOALS

ROUTE

MILESTONES & STOPS	TIME OF ARRIVAL	HIGHLIGHTS & NOTES

ADDITIONAL NOTES

DATE

STARTING POINT

DESTINATION

DISTANCE

DURATION

WEATHER CONDITIONS

WATER VISIBILITY

CLEAR 1 2 3 4 5 MISTY

TEAM / PADDLE PARTNER

•	•
•	•
•	•

BODY OF WATER

LAKE	RIVER	CANAL
SEA	OCEAN	OTHER

GEAR & EQUIPMENT

TRIP GOALS

ROUTE

MILESTONES & STOPS	TIME OF ARRIVAL	HIGHLIGHTS & NOTES

ADDITIONAL NOTES

DATE

STARTING POINT

DESTINATION

DISTANCE

DURATION

WEATHER CONDITIONS

WATER VISIBILITY

| CLEAR | 1 | 2 | 3 | 4 | 5 | MISTY |

TEAM / PADDLE PARTNER

•	•
•	•
•	•

BODY OF WATER

☐ LAKE	☐ RIVER	☐ CANAL
☐ SEA	☐ OCEAN	☐ OTHER

GEAR & EQUIPMENT

TRIP GOALS

ROUTE

MILESTONES & STOPS	TIME OF ARRIVAL	HIGHLIGHTS & NOTES

ADDITIONAL NOTES

DATE

STARTING POINT

DESTINATION

DISTANCE

DURATION

WEATHER CONDITIONS

WATER VISIBILITY

| CLEAR | 1 | 2 | 3 | 4 | 5 | MISTY |

TEAM / PADDLE PARTNER

•	•
•	•
•	•

BODY OF WATER

☐ LAKE	☐ RIVER	☐ CANAL
☐ SEA	☐ OCEAN	☐ OTHER

GEAR & EQUIPMENT

TRIP GOALS

ROUTE

MILESTONES & STOPS	TIME OF ARRIVAL	HIGHLIGHTS & NOTES

ADDITIONAL NOTES

DATE

STARTING POINT

DESTINATION

DISTANCE

DURATION

WEATHER CONDITIONS

WATER VISIBILITY

	1	2	3	4	5	
CLEAR	○	○	○	○	○	MISTY

TEAM / PADDLE PARTNER

·	·
·	·
·	·

BODY OF WATER

☐ LAKE	☐ RIVER	☐ CANAL
☐ SEA	☐ OCEAN	☐ OTHER

GEAR & EQUIPMENT

TRIP GOALS

ROUTE

MILESTONES & STOPS	TIME OF ARRIVAL	HIGHLIGHTS & NOTES

ADDITIONAL NOTES

DATE

STARTING POINT

DESTINATION

DISTANCE

DURATION

WEATHER CONDITIONS

☀ 🌤 🌧 ⛈ ❄

WATER VISIBILITY

| CLEAR | 1 | 2 | 3 | 4 | 5 | MISTY |

TEAM / PADDLE PARTNER

•	•
•	•
•	•

BODY OF WATER

☐ LAKE	☐ RIVER	☐ CANAL
☐ SEA	☐ OCEAN	☐ OTHER

GEAR & EQUIPMENT

TRIP GOALS

ROUTE

MILESTONES & STOPS	TIME OF ARRIVAL	HIGHLIGHTS & NOTES

ADDITIONAL NOTES

	DATE
	STARTING POINT
	DESTINATION
	DISTANCE
	DURATION

WEATHER CONDITIONS

WATER VISIBILITY

CLEAR 1 2 3 4 5 MISTY

TEAM / PADDLE PARTNER

•	•
•	•
•	•

BODY OF WATER

☐ LAKE	☐ RIVER	☐ CANAL
☐ SEA	☐ OCEAN	☐ OTHER

GEAR & EQUIPMENT

TRIP GOALS

ROUTE

⚑ MILESTONES & STOPS	⏱ TIME OF ARRIVAL	☆ HIGHLIGHTS & NOTES

ADDITIONAL NOTES

DATE

STARTING POINT

DESTINATION

DISTANCE

DURATION

WEATHER CONDITIONS

WATER VISIBILITY

CLEAR 1   2   3   4   5 MISTY

TEAM / PADDLE PARTNER

•	•
•	•
•	•

BODY OF WATER

LAKE	RIVER	CANAL
SEA	OCEAN	OTHER

GEAR & EQUIPMENT

TRIP GOALS

ROUTE

MILESTONES & STOPS	TIME OF ARRIVAL	HIGHLIGHTS & NOTES

ADDITIONAL NOTES

📅 DATE	
🧭 STARTING POINT	
🚩 DESTINATION	
📍 DISTANCE	
⏱️ DURATION	

WEATHER CONDITIONS

🌡️ _____ ☀️ ⛅ 🌧️ ⛈️ ❄️

🚩 _____ ☐ ☐ ☐ ☐ ☐

WATER VISIBILITY

☀️ 1 2 3 4 5 ☁️
CLEAR ◯ ◯ ◯ ◯ ◯ MISTY

TEAM / PADDLE PARTNER

·	·
·	·
·	·

BODY OF WATER

☐ LAKE	☐ RIVER	☐ CANAL
☐ SEA	☐ OCEAN	☐ OTHER

GEAR & EQUIPMENT

TRIP GOALS

ROUTE

🏁 MILESTONES & STOPS	🕐 TIME OF ARRIVAL	⭐ HIGHLIGHTS & NOTES

ADDITIONAL NOTES

	DATE
	STARTING POINT
	DESTINATION
	DISTANCE
	DURATION

WEATHER CONDITIONS

		☀	⛅	☁	🌧	❄
	—	☐	☐	☐	☐	☐

WATER VISIBILITY

CLEAR 1 2 3 4 5 MISTY

TEAM / PADDLE PARTNER

•	•
•	•
•	•

BODY OF WATER

☐ LAKE	☐ RIVER	☐ CANAL
☐ SEA	☐ OCEAN	☐ OTHER

GEAR & EQUIPMENT

TRIP GOALS

ROUTE

MILESTONES & STOPS	TIME OF ARRIVAL	HIGHLIGHTS & NOTES

ADDITIONAL NOTES

DATE

STARTING POINT

DESTINATION

DISTANCE

DURATION

WEATHER CONDITIONS

WATER VISIBILITY

CLEAR 1 2 3 4 5 MISTY

TEAM / PADDLE PARTNER

•	•
•	•
•	•

BODY OF WATER

☐ LAKE	☐ RIVER	☐ CANAL
☐ SEA	☐ OCEAN	☐ OTHER

GEAR & EQUIPMENT

TRIP GOALS

ROUTE

MILESTONES & STOPS	TIME OF ARRIVAL	HIGHLIGHTS & NOTES

ADDITIONAL NOTES

DATE

STARTING POINT

DESTINATION

DISTANCE

DURATION

WEATHER CONDITIONS

WATER VISIBILITY

CLEAR	1	2	3	4	5	MISTY

TEAM / PADDLE PARTNER

·	·
·	·
·	·

BODY OF WATER

☐ LAKE	☐ RIVER	☐ CANAL
☐ SEA	☐ OCEAN	☐ OTHER

GEAR & EQUIPMENT

TRIP GOALS

ROUTE

MILESTONES & STOPS	TIME OF ARRIVAL	HIGHLIGHTS & NOTES

ADDITIONAL NOTES

	DATE
	STARTING POINT
	DESTINATION
	DISTANCE
	DURATION

WEATHER CONDITIONS

☀ ⛅ ☁ ⛈ ❄

☐ ☐ ☐ ☐ ☐

WATER VISIBILITY

CLEAR 1 2 3 4 5 MISTY
○ ○ ○ ○ ○

TEAM / PADDLE PARTNER

•	•
•	•
•	•

BODY OF WATER

☐ LAKE	☐ RIVER	☐ CANAL
☐ SEA	☐ OCEAN	☐ OTHER

GEAR & EQUIPMENT

TRIP GOALS

ROUTE

MILESTONES & STOPS	TIME OF ARRIVAL	HIGHLIGHTS & NOTES

ADDITIONAL NOTES

DATE

STARTING POINT

DESTINATION

DISTANCE

DURATION

WEATHER CONDITIONS

WATER VISIBILITY

CLEAR 1 2 3 4 5 MISTY

TEAM / PADDLE PARTNER

•	•
•	•
•	•

BODY OF WATER

☐ LAKE	☐ RIVER	☐ CANAL
☐ SEA	☐ OCEAN	☐ OTHER

GEAR & EQUIPMENT

TRIP GOALS

ROUTE

MILESTONES & STOPS	TIME OF ARRIVAL	HIGHLIGHTS & NOTES

ADDITIONAL NOTES

	DATE
	STARTING POINT
	DESTINATION
	DISTANCE
	DURATION

WEATHER CONDITIONS

🌡 _____ ☀ ⛅ 🌧 ⛈ ❄

🚩 _____ ☐ ☐ ☐ ☐ ☐

WATER VISIBILITY

CLEAR 1 2 3 4 5 MISTY
○ ○ ○ ○ ○

TEAM / PADDLE PARTNER

•	•
•	•
•	•

BODY OF WATER

☐ LAKE	☐ RIVER	☐ CANAL
☐ SEA	☐ OCEAN	☐ OTHER

GEAR & EQUIPMENT

TRIP GOALS

ROUTE

MILESTONES & STOPS	TIME OF ARRIVAL	HIGHLIGHTS & NOTES

ADDITIONAL NOTES

	DATE
	STARTING POINT
	DESTINATION
	DISTANCE
	DURATION

WEATHER CONDITIONS

WATER VISIBILITY

CLEAR 1 2 3 4 5 MISTY

TEAM / PADDLE PARTNER

.	.
.	.
.	.

BODY OF WATER

LAKE	RIVER	CANAL
SEA	OCEAN	OTHER

GEAR & EQUIPMENT

TRIP GOALS

ROUTE

MILESTONES & STOPS	TIME OF ARRIVAL	HIGHLIGHTS & NOTES

ADDITIONAL NOTES

	DATE
	STARTING POINT
	DESTINATION
	DISTANCE
	DURATION

WEATHER CONDITIONS

☀ ⛅ ☁ ⛈ ❄

☐ ☐ ☐ ☐ ☐

WATER VISIBILITY

CLEAR 1 2 3 4 5 MISTY
☐ ☐ ☐ ☐ ☐

TEAM / PADDLE PARTNER

•	•
•	•
•	•

BODY OF WATER

☐ LAKE	☐ RIVER	☐ CANAL
☐ SEA	☐ OCEAN	☐ OTHER

GEAR & EQUIPMENT

TRIP GOALS

ROUTE

MILESTONES & STOPS	TIME OF ARRIVAL	HIGHLIGHTS & NOTES

ADDITIONAL NOTES

DATE

STARTING POINT

DESTINATION

DISTANCE

DURATION

WEATHER CONDITIONS

WATER VISIBILITY

	1	2	3	4	5	
CLEAR	○	○	○	○	○	MISTY

TEAM / PADDLE PARTNER

•	•
•	•
•	•

BODY OF WATER

☐ LAKE	☐ RIVER	☐ CANAL
☐ SEA	☐ OCEAN	☐ OTHER

GEAR & EQUIPMENT

TRIP GOALS

ROUTE

MILESTONES & STOPS	TIME OF ARRIVAL	HIGHLIGHTS & NOTES

ADDITIONAL NOTES

📅 **DATE**	
⬥ **STARTING POINT**	
🚩 **DESTINATION**	
📍 **DISTANCE**	
⏱ **DURATION**	

WEATHER CONDITIONS

🌡 _____ ☀️ ⛅ ☁️ 🌧 ❄️

🎐 _____ ☐ ☐ ☐ ☐ ☐

WATER VISIBILITY

CLEAR 1 2 3 4 5 MISTY

TEAM / PADDLE PARTNER

•	•
•	•
•	•

BODY OF WATER

☐ LAKE	☐ RIVER	☐ CANAL
☐ SEA	☐ OCEAN	☐ OTHER

GEAR & EQUIPMENT

TRIP GOALS

ROUTE

🚩 MILESTONES & STOPS	⏰ TIME OF ARRIVAL	⭐ HIGHLIGHTS & NOTES

ADDITIONAL NOTES

DATE

STARTING POINT

DESTINATION

DISTANCE

DURATION

WEATHER CONDITIONS

WATER VISIBILITY

CLEAR 1 2 3 4 5 MISTY

TEAM / PADDLE PARTNER

.	.
.	.
.	.

BODY OF WATER

☐ LAKE	☐ RIVER	☐ CANAL
☐ SEA	☐ OCEAN	☐ OTHER

GEAR & EQUIPMENT

TRIP GOALS

ROUTE

MILESTONES & STOPS	TIME OF ARRIVAL	HIGHLIGHTS & NOTES

ADDITIONAL NOTES

📅 **DATE**	
🧭 **STARTING POINT**	
🚩 **DESTINATION**	
📍 **DISTANCE**	
⏱ **DURATION**	

WEATHER CONDITIONS

🌡 ____ ☀️ ⛅ ☁️ 🌧 ❄️

🌬 ____ ☐ ☐ ☐ ☐ ☐

WATER VISIBILITY

☀️ 1 2 3 4 5 🌫

CLEAR ◯ ◯ ◯ ◯ ◯ MISTY

TEAM / PADDLE PARTNER

•	•
•	•
•	•

BODY OF WATER

☐ LAKE	☐ RIVER	☐ CANAL
☐ SEA	☐ OCEAN	☐ OTHER

GEAR & EQUIPMENT

TRIP GOALS

ROUTE

📍 MILESTONES & STOPS	🕐 TIME OF ARRIVAL	⭐ HIGHLIGHTS & NOTES

ADDITIONAL NOTES

DATE

STARTING POINT

DESTINATION

DISTANCE

DURATION

WEATHER CONDITIONS

WATER VISIBILITY

CLEAR 1 2 3 4 5 MISTY

TEAM / PADDLE PARTNER

•	•
•	•
•	•

BODY OF WATER

☐ LAKE	☐ RIVER	☐ CANAL
☐ SEA	☐ OCEAN	☐ OTHER

GEAR & EQUIPMENT

TRIP GOALS

ROUTE

MILESTONES & STOPS	TIME OF ARRIVAL	HIGHLIGHTS & NOTES

ADDITIONAL NOTES

📅 **DATE**	
🧭 **STARTING POINT**	
🚩 **DESTINATION**	
📍 **DISTANCE**	
⏱️ **DURATION**	

WEATHER CONDITIONS

🌡️ _____ ☀️ ⛅ ☁️ 🌧️ ❄️

🌬️ _____ ☐ ☐ ☐ ☐ ☐

WATER VISIBILITY

☀️ CLEAR   1 ◯   2 ◯   3 ◯   4 ◯   5 ◯   🌫️ MISTY

TEAM / PADDLE PARTNER

•	•
•	•
•	•

BODY OF WATER

☐ LAKE	☐ RIVER	☐ CANAL
☐ SEA	☐ OCEAN	☐ OTHER

GEAR & EQUIPMENT

TRIP GOALS

ROUTE

🚩 MILESTONES & STOPS	🕐 TIME OF ARRIVAL	⭐ HIGHLIGHTS & NOTES

ADDITIONAL NOTES

📅 **DATE**	
🛶 **STARTING POINT**	
🚩 **DESTINATION**	
📍 **DISTANCE**	
⏱ **DURATION**	

WEATHER CONDITIONS

🌡 ____ ☀️ ⛅ 🌧 ⛈ ❄️

🌬 ____ ☐ ☐ ☐ ☐ ☐

WATER VISIBILITY

☀️ 1   2   3   4   5 ☁️
CLEAR ◯   ◯   ◯   ◯   ◯ MISTY

TEAM / PADDLE PARTNER

•	•
•	•
•	•

BODY OF WATER

☐ LAKE	☐ RIVER	☐ CANAL
☐ SEA	☐ OCEAN	☐ OTHER

GEAR & EQUIPMENT

TRIP GOALS

ROUTE

📍 MILESTONES & STOPS	🕐 TIME OF ARRIVAL	⭐ HIGHLIGHTS & NOTES

ADDITIONAL NOTES

DATE	
STARTING POINT	
DESTINATION	
DISTANCE	
DURATION	

WEATHER CONDITIONS

☀ 🌤 🌧 ⛈ ❄

☐ ☐ ☐ ☐ ☐

WATER VISIBILITY

CLEAR 1 2 3 4 5 MISTY

TEAM / PADDLE PARTNER

•	•
•	•
•	•

BODY OF WATER

☐ LAKE	☐ RIVER	☐ CANAL
☐ SEA	☐ OCEAN	☐ OTHER

GEAR & EQUIPMENT

TRIP GOALS

ROUTE

MILESTONES & STOPS	TIME OF ARRIVAL	HIGHLIGHTS & NOTES

ADDITIONAL NOTES

DATE

STARTING POINT

DESTINATION

DISTANCE

DURATION

WEATHER CONDITIONS

☀ ⛅ ☁ ⛈ ❄

☐ ☐ ☐ ☐ ☐

WATER VISIBILITY

CLEAR 1 2 3 4 5 MISTY

◯ ◯ ◯ ◯ ◯

TEAM / PADDLE PARTNER

•	•
•	•
•	•

BODY OF WATER

☐ LAKE	☐ RIVER	☐ CANAL
☐ SEA	☐ OCEAN	☐ OTHER

GEAR & EQUIPMENT

TRIP GOALS

ROUTE

MILESTONES & STOPS	TIME OF ARRIVAL	HIGHLIGHTS & NOTES

ADDITIONAL NOTES

DATE

STARTING POINT

DESTINATION

DISTANCE

DURATION

WEATHER CONDITIONS

WATER VISIBILITY

| CLEAR | 1 | 2 | 3 | 4 | 5 | MISTY |

TEAM / PADDLE PARTNER

•	•
•	•
•	•

BODY OF WATER

☐ LAKE	☐ RIVER	☐ CANAL
☐ SEA	☐ OCEAN	☐ OTHER

GEAR & EQUIPMENT

TRIP GOALS

ROUTE

⚑ MILESTONES & STOPS	🕐 TIME OF ARRIVAL	☆ HIGHLIGHTS & NOTES

ADDITIONAL NOTES

DATE	
STARTING POINT	
DESTINATION	
DISTANCE	
DURATION	

WEATHER CONDITIONS

temperature: ____ ☀ ⛅ ☁ ⛈ ❄

wind: ____ ☐ ☐ ☐ ☐ ☐

WATER VISIBILITY

CLEAR 1 2 3 4 5 MISTY

TEAM / PADDLE PARTNER

•	•
•	•
•	•

BODY OF WATER

☐ LAKE	☐ RIVER	☐ CANAL
☐ SEA	☐ OCEAN	☐ OTHER

GEAR & EQUIPMENT

TRIP GOALS

ROUTE

MILESTONES & STOPS	TIME OF ARRIVAL	HIGHLIGHTS & NOTES

ADDITIONAL NOTES

DATE

STARTING POINT

DESTINATION

DISTANCE

DURATION

WEATHER CONDITIONS

WATER VISIBILITY

CLEAR 1 2 3 4 5 MISTY

TEAM / PADDLE PARTNER

•	•
•	•
•	•

BODY OF WATER

☐ LAKE	☐ RIVER	☐ CANAL
☐ SEA	☐ OCEAN	☐ OTHER

GEAR & EQUIPMENT

TRIP GOALS

ROUTE

MILESTONES & STOPS	TIME OF ARRIVAL	HIGHLIGHTS & NOTES

ADDITIONAL NOTES

DATE

STARTING POINT

DESTINATION

DISTANCE

DURATION

WEATHER CONDITIONS

☀ ⛅ ☁ ⛈ ❄

☐ ☐ ☐ ☐ ☐

WATER VISIBILITY

CLEAR 1 2 3 4 5 MISTY
○ ○ ○ ○ ○

TEAM / PADDLE PARTNER

•	•
•	•
•	•

BODY OF WATER

☐ LAKE	☐ RIVER	☐ CANAL
☐ SEA	☐ OCEAN	☐ OTHER

GEAR & EQUIPMENT

TRIP GOALS

ROUTE

MILESTONES & STOPS	TIME OF ARRIVAL	HIGHLIGHTS & NOTES

ADDITIONAL NOTES

📅 **DATE**	
🛶 **STARTING POINT**	
🚩 **DESTINATION**	
📍 **DISTANCE**	
⏱ **DURATION**	

WEATHER CONDITIONS

🌡 ___ ☀️ ⛅ 🌧 ⛈ ❄️

💨 ___ ☐ ☐ ☐ ☐ ☐

WATER VISIBILITY

☀️ 1 2 3 4 5 ☁️
CLEAR ◯ ◯ ◯ ◯ ◯ MISTY

TEAM / PADDLE PARTNER

•	•
•	•
•	•

BODY OF WATER

☐ LAKE	☐ RIVER	☐ CANAL
☐ SEA	☐ OCEAN	☐ OTHER

GEAR & EQUIPMENT

TRIP GOALS

ROUTE

📍 MILESTONES & STOPS	🕐 TIME OF ARRIVAL	⭐ HIGHLIGHTS & NOTES

ADDITIONAL NOTES

DATE

STARTING POINT

DESTINATION

DISTANCE

DURATION

WEATHER CONDITIONS

WATER VISIBILITY

CLEAR   1   2   3   4   5   MISTY

TEAM / PADDLE PARTNER

•	•
•	•
•	•

BODY OF WATER

☐ LAKE	☐ RIVER	☐ CANAL
☐ SEA	☐ OCEAN	☐ OTHER

GEAR & EQUIPMENT

TRIP GOALS

ROUTE

🚩 MILESTONES & STOPS	🕐 TIME OF ARRIVAL	☆ HIGHLIGHTS & NOTES

ADDITIONAL NOTES

DATE	
STARTING POINT	
DESTINATION	
DISTANCE	
DURATION	

WEATHER CONDITIONS

☀ ⛅ ☁ ⛈ ❄

☐ ☐ ☐ ☐ ☐

WATER VISIBILITY

CLEAR 1 2 3 4 5 MISTY

TEAM / PADDLE PARTNER

•	•
•	•
•	•

BODY OF WATER

☐ LAKE	☐ RIVER	☐ CANAL
☐ SEA	☐ OCEAN	☐ OTHER

GEAR & EQUIPMENT

TRIP GOALS

ROUTE

MILESTONES & STOPS	TIME OF ARRIVAL	HIGHLIGHTS & NOTES

ADDITIONAL NOTES

DATE

STARTING POINT

DESTINATION

DISTANCE

DURATION

WEATHER CONDITIONS

WATER VISIBILITY

CLEAR 1 2 3 4 5 MISTY

TEAM / PADDLE PARTNER

•	•
•	•
•	•

BODY OF WATER

LAKE	RIVER	CANAL
SEA	OCEAN	OTHER

GEAR & EQUIPMENT

TRIP GOALS

ROUTE

MILESTONES & STOPS	TIME OF ARRIVAL	HIGHLIGHTS & NOTES

ADDITIONAL NOTES

DATE

STARTING POINT

DESTINATION

DISTANCE

DURATION

WEATHER CONDITIONS

WATER VISIBILITY

CLEAR 1 2 3 4 5 MISTY

TEAM / PADDLE PARTNER

•	•
•	•
•	•

BODY OF WATER

☐ LAKE	☐ RIVER	☐ CANAL
☐ SEA	☐ OCEAN	☐ OTHER

GEAR & EQUIPMENT

TRIP GOALS

ROUTE

🚩 MILESTONES & STOPS	🕐 TIME OF ARRIVAL	☆ HIGHLIGHTS & NOTES

ADDITIONAL NOTES

DATE

STARTING POINT

DESTINATION

DISTANCE

DURATION

WEATHER CONDITIONS

WATER VISIBILITY

CLEAR | 1 | 2 | 3 | 4 | 5 | MISTY

TEAM / PADDLE PARTNER

•	•
•	•
•	•

BODY OF WATER

☐ LAKE	☐ RIVER	☐ CANAL
☐ SEA	☐ OCEAN	☐ OTHER

GEAR & EQUIPMENT

TRIP GOALS

ROUTE

MILESTONES & STOPS	TIME OF ARRIVAL	HIGHLIGHTS & NOTES

ADDITIONAL NOTES

DATE		WEATHER CONDITIONS					

DATE

STARTING POINT

DESTINATION

DISTANCE

DURATION

WEATHER CONDITIONS

WATER VISIBILITY

CLEAR 1 2 3 4 5 MISTY

TEAM / PADDLE PARTNER

•	•
•	•
•	•

BODY OF WATER

☐ LAKE	☐ RIVER	☐ CANAL
☐ SEA	☐ OCEAN	☐ OTHER

GEAR & EQUIPMENT

TRIP GOALS

ROUTE

MILESTONES & STOPS	TIME OF ARRIVAL	HIGHLIGHTS & NOTES

ADDITIONAL NOTES

DATE

STARTING POINT

DESTINATION

DISTANCE

DURATION

WEATHER CONDITIONS

WATER VISIBILITY

CLEAR 1 2 3 4 5 MISTY

TEAM / PADDLE PARTNER

•	•
•	•
•	•

BODY OF WATER

☐ LAKE	☐ RIVER	☐ CANAL
☐ SEA	☐ OCEAN	☐ OTHER

GEAR & EQUIPMENT

TRIP GOALS

ROUTE

MILESTONES & STOPS	TIME OF ARRIVAL	HIGHLIGHTS & NOTES

ADDITIONAL NOTES

📅 **DATE**	
🚣 **STARTING POINT**	
🚩 **DESTINATION**	
📍 **DISTANCE**	
⏱️ **DURATION**	

WEATHER CONDITIONS

🌡️ _____ ☀️ ⛅ 🌧️ ⛈️ ❄️

🎐 _____ ☐ ☐ ☐ ☐ ☐

WATER VISIBILITY

☀️ 1   2   3   4   5 ☁️
CLEAR ○   ○   ○   ○   ○ MISTY

TEAM / PADDLE PARTNER

•	•
•	•
•	•

BODY OF WATER

☐ LAKE	☐ RIVER	☐ CANAL
☐ SEA	☐ OCEAN	☐ OTHER

GEAR & EQUIPMENT

TRIP GOALS

ROUTE

🏁 MILESTONES & STOPS	🕐 TIME OF ARRIVAL	☆ HIGHLIGHTS & NOTES

ADDITIONAL NOTES

DATE

STARTING POINT

DESTINATION

DISTANCE

DURATION

WEATHER CONDITIONS

WATER VISIBILITY

CLEAR 1 2 3 4 5 MISTY

TEAM / PADDLE PARTNER

•	•
•	•
•	•

BODY OF WATER

LAKE	RIVER	CANAL
SEA	OCEAN	OTHER

GEAR & EQUIPMENT

TRIP GOALS

ROUTE

MILESTONES & STOPS	TIME OF ARRIVAL	HIGHLIGHTS & NOTES

ADDITIONAL NOTES

	DATE	
	STARTING POINT	
	DESTINATION	
	DISTANCE	
	DURATION	

WEATHER CONDITIONS

🌡 _____   ☀ ⛅ ☁ ⛈ ❄

💨 _____   ☐ ☐ ☐ ☐ ☐

WATER VISIBILITY

☀ CLEAR   1   2   3   4   5   MISTY ☁

TEAM / PADDLE PARTNER

•	•
•	•
•	•

BODY OF WATER

☐ LAKE	☐ RIVER	☐ CANAL
☐ SEA	☐ OCEAN	☐ OTHER

GEAR & EQUIPMENT

TRIP GOALS

ROUTE

MILESTONES & STOPS	TIME OF ARRIVAL	HIGHLIGHTS & NOTES

ADDITIONAL NOTES

DATE

STARTING POINT

DESTINATION

DISTANCE

DURATION

WEATHER CONDITIONS

		☀	⛅	🌧	⛈	❄
		☐	☐	☐	☐	☐

WATER VISIBILITY

CLEAR 1 2 3 4 5 MISTY

TEAM / PADDLE PARTNER

·	·
·	·
·	·

BODY OF WATER

☐ LAKE	☐ RIVER	☐ CANAL
☐ SEA	☐ OCEAN	☐ OTHER

GEAR & EQUIPMENT

TRIP GOALS

ROUTE

⚐ MILESTONES & STOPS	⏱ TIME OF ARRIVAL	☆ HIGHLIGHTS & NOTES

ADDITIONAL NOTES

DATE

STARTING POINT

DESTINATION

DISTANCE

DURATION

WEATHER CONDITIONS

WATER VISIBILITY

CLEAR 1 2 3 4 5 MISTY

TEAM / PADDLE PARTNER

•	•
•	•
•	•

BODY OF WATER

☐ LAKE	☐ RIVER	☐ CANAL
☐ SEA	☐ OCEAN	☐ OTHER

GEAR & EQUIPMENT

TRIP GOALS

ROUTE

MILESTONES & STOPS	TIME OF ARRIVAL	HIGHLIGHTS & NOTES

ADDITIONAL NOTES

DATE

STARTING POINT

DESTINATION

DISTANCE

DURATION

WEATHER CONDITIONS

WATER VISIBILITY

CLEAR 1 2 3 4 5 MISTY

TEAM / PADDLE PARTNER

·	·
·	·
·	·

BODY OF WATER

| LAKE | RIVER | CANAL |
| SEA | OCEAN | OTHER |

GEAR & EQUIPMENT

TRIP GOALS

ROUTE

MILESTONES & STOPS	TIME OF ARRIVAL	HIGHLIGHTS & NOTES

ADDITIONAL NOTES

DATE

STARTING POINT

DESTINATION

DISTANCE

DURATION

WEATHER CONDITIONS

WATER VISIBILITY

CLEAR   1   2   3   4   5   MISTY

TEAM / PADDLE PARTNER

•	•
•	•
•	•

BODY OF WATER

☐ LAKE	☐ RIVER	☐ CANAL
☐ SEA	☐ OCEAN	☐ OTHER

GEAR & EQUIPMENT

TRIP GOALS

ROUTE

MILESTONES & STOPS	TIME OF ARRIVAL	HIGHLIGHTS & NOTES

ADDITIONAL NOTES

Made in the USA
Columbia, SC
20 April 2022